APRIL
Unwrapped

My Naked Dreams Revealed

April Brucker

Publisher: CFBP Bestsellers
An imprint of CFB Productions Inc.
P. O. Box 50008, Henderson, NV 89016
www.CFBPBestsellers.com

FOREWORD

Nightmares are where we often confront our greatest fears. A while back, I had recurring dreams where I was naked in public. I was just minding my own business, doing everyday tasks. Then, BLAMO! My clothes were gone.

AHHHHHH!!!!!

The last straw was when I was performing standup in a comedy club and my clothes completely disappeared. The audience was laughing, but were they laughing at my punchline or my waistline?

I needed answers. So, I went to a tenth-generation psychic who gave me a tarot card reading. The cards revealed that by tapping into my imagination, I would overcome my fears.

April Unwrapped was born.

In this book, I have confronted not only my insecurities, but more impotantly the insecurities that we all face. We all fear being caught naked by an unsuspecting person. In our dreams, we fear suddenly being naked in public. Many performers even fear finding themselves completely naked on air, on screen or on stage. It's our own personal version of *The Emperor's New Clothes.*

In the Western World, we have issues when it comes to sex and sexuality. We shame people for their body size and shape. We destroy someone for not being mainstream beautiful. We bully others based on their appearance.

In a world where so many tear others down to build themselves up, can you blame people for wanting to keep their clothes on?

In this body-positive, feminist-affirming book, I reveal my art as well as my heart. I invite you not only to share my naked dreams, but also to perhaps consider getting unwrapped yourself sometime.

Always Dream!

April

I dreamed
you popped my
champagne in
January.
Cheers!
April

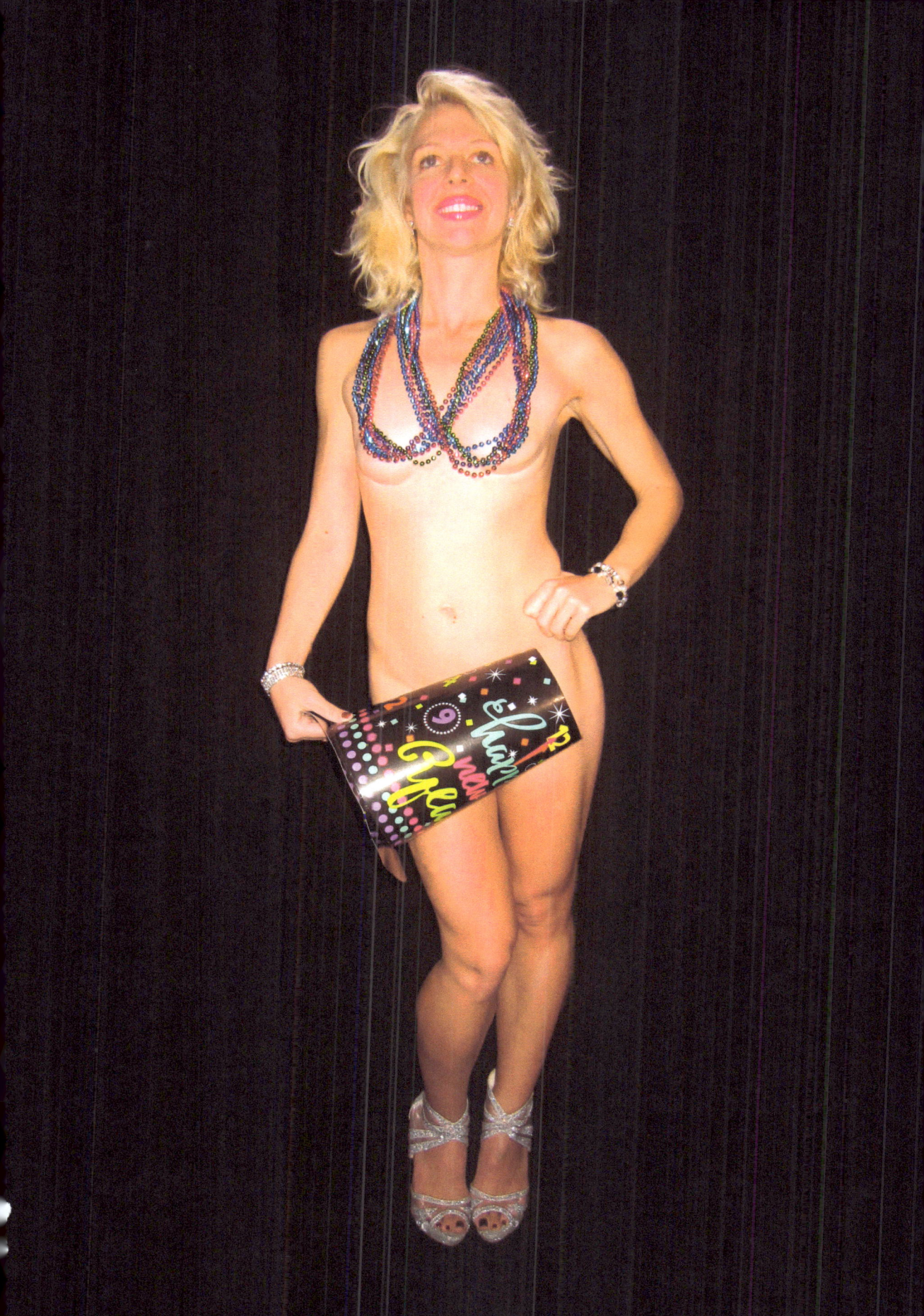

I dreamed
you wanted
my sweets in
February.
Xoxo!
April

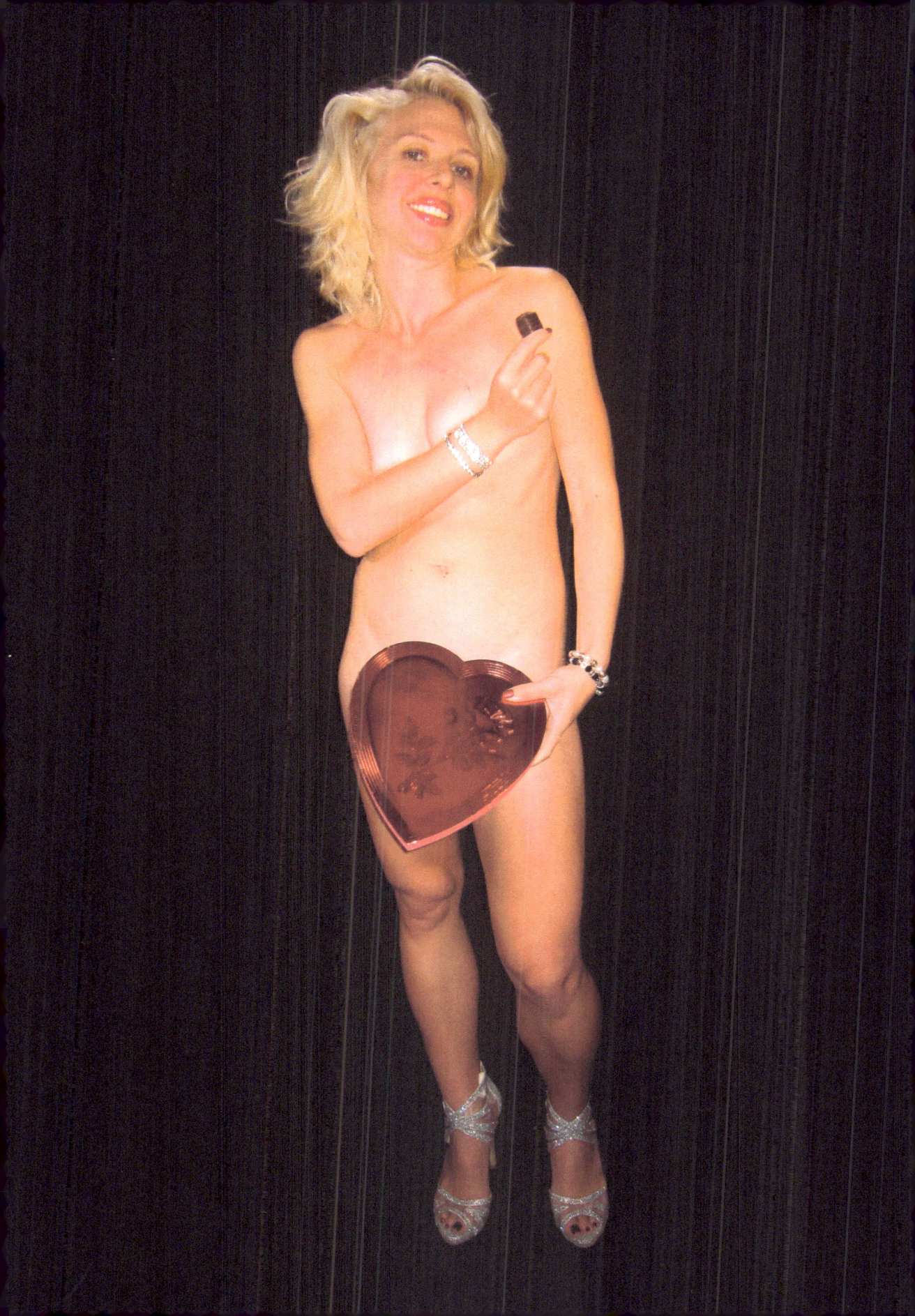

I dreamed you wanted to light up in March. Hugs! April

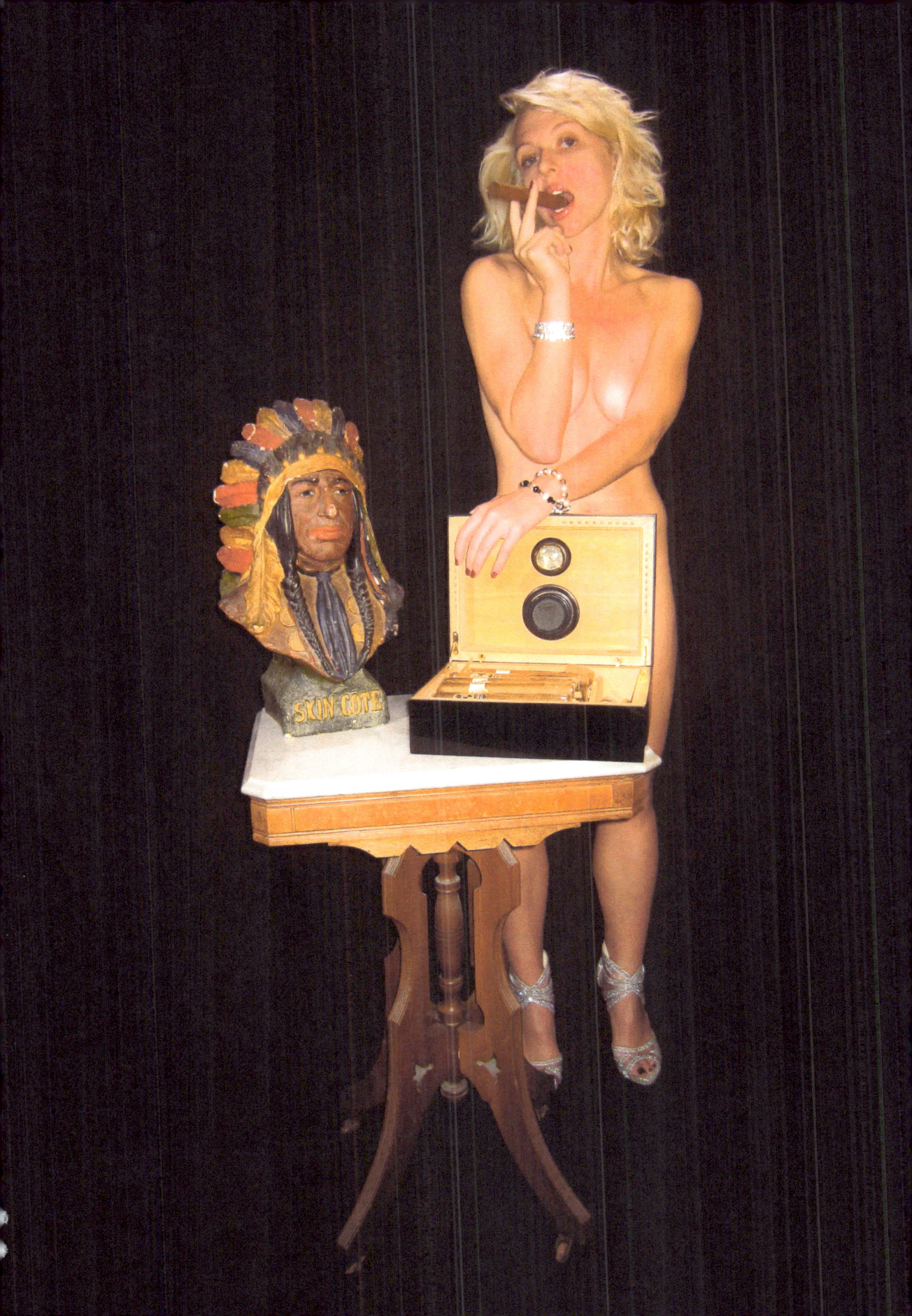

I dreamed
you liked
April showers.
Stay Cool!
April

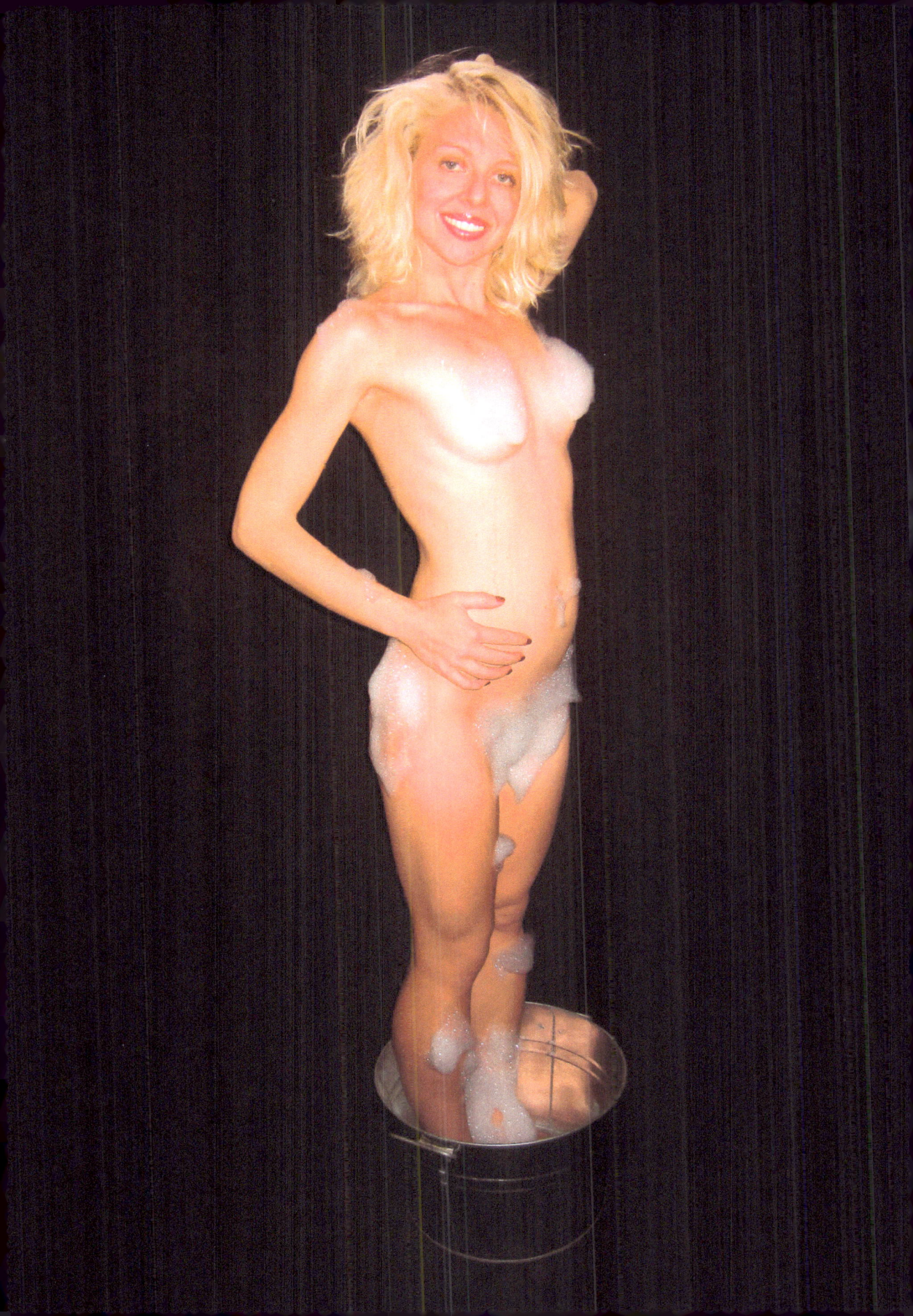

I dreamed
you planted my
May flowers.
Au Revoir!
April

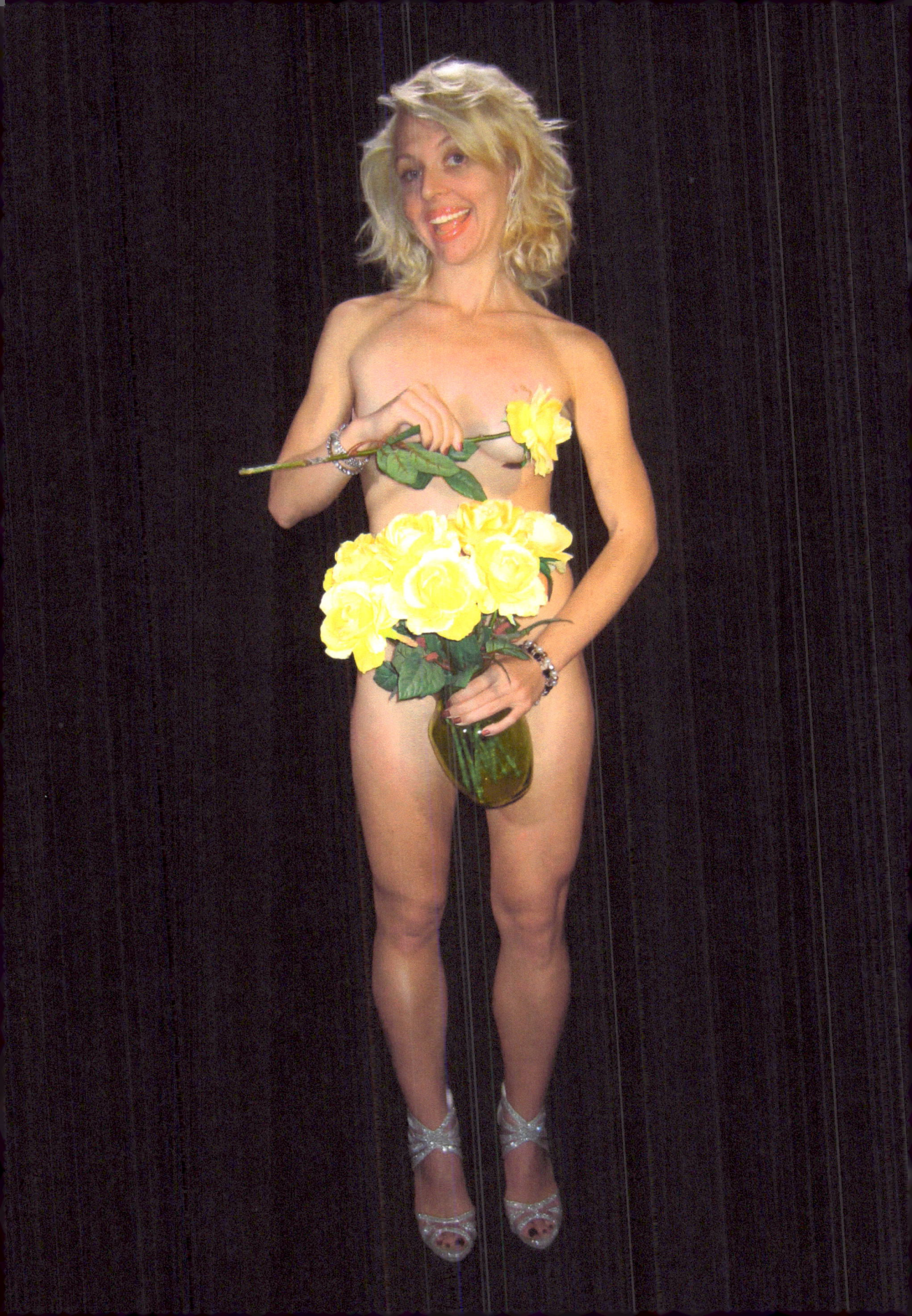

I dreamed
you shared my
basket in June.
Keep Smiling!
April

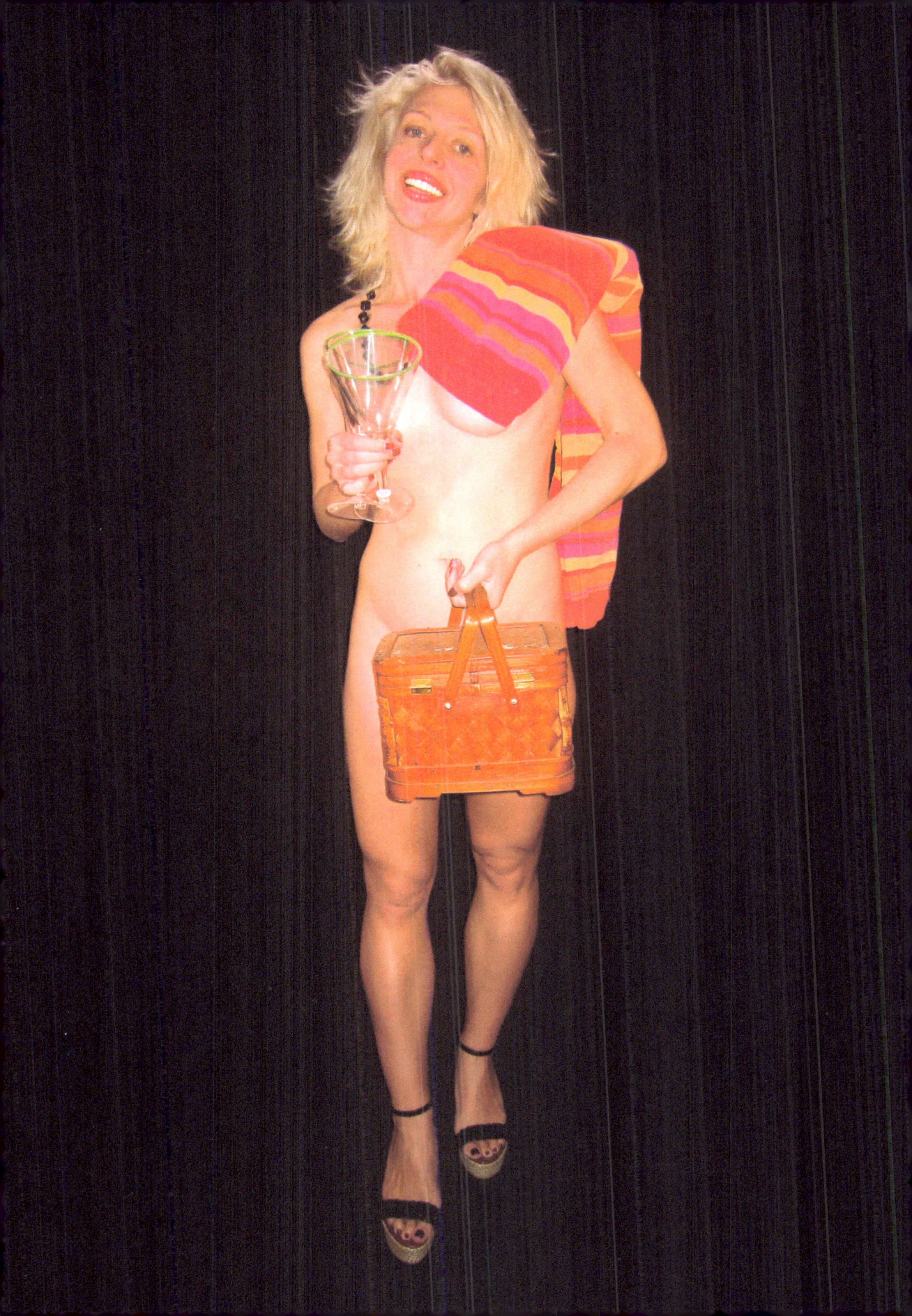

I dreamed
you wanted to
take a dip in July.
Bubbly!
April

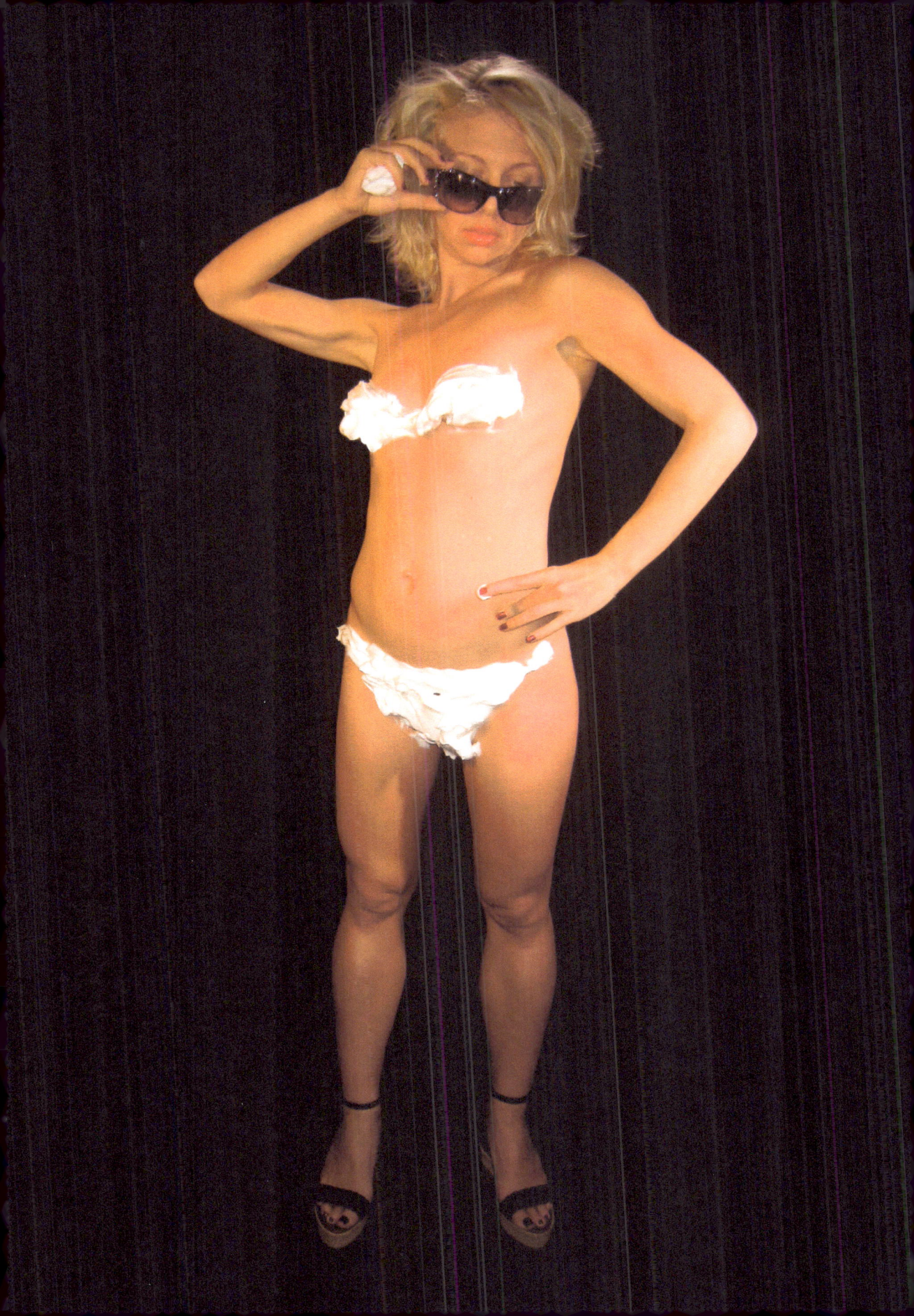

I dreamed
you wanted to
savor my wine
in August.
Besos Mi Amor!
April

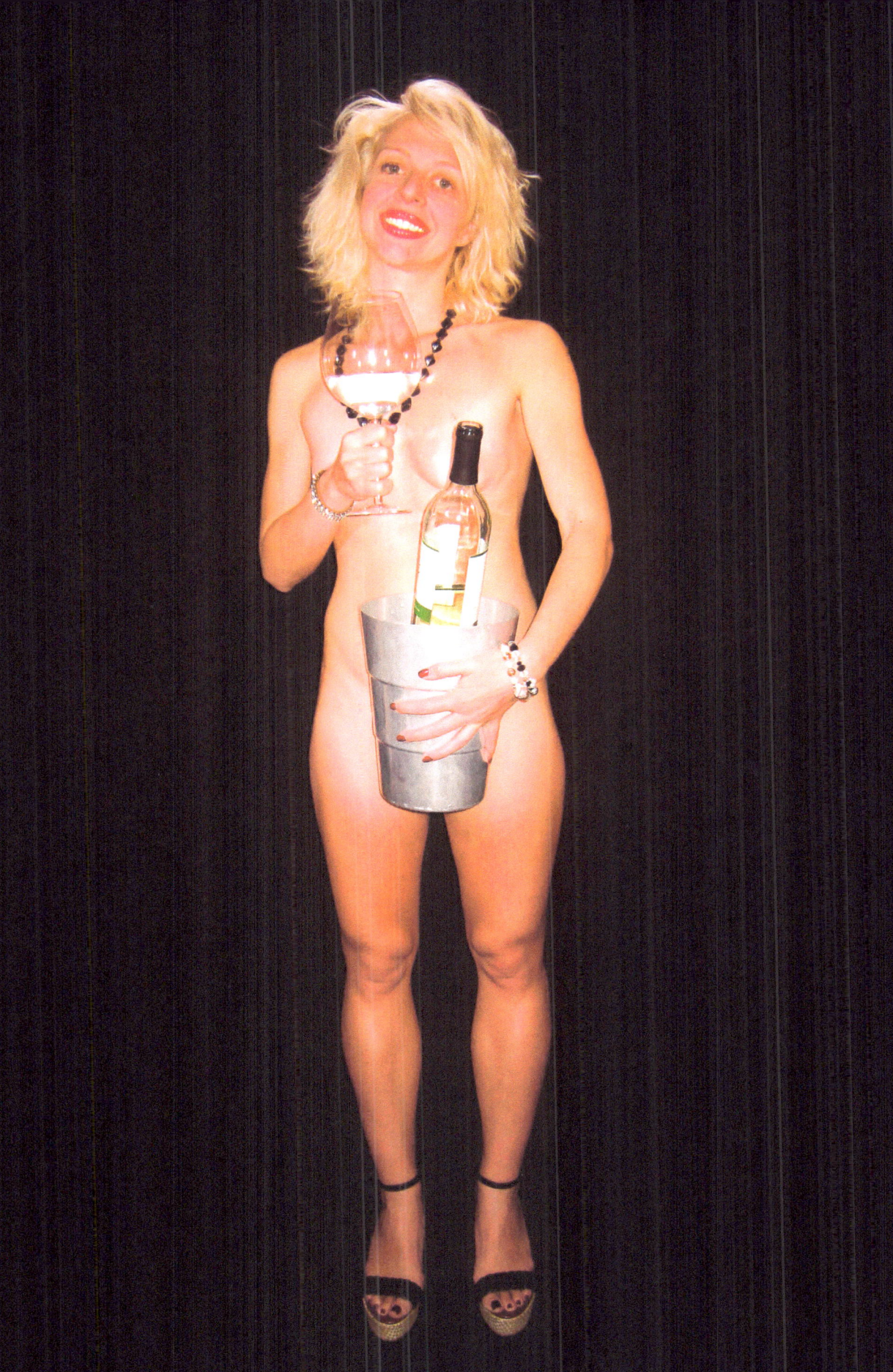

I dreamed
you showed me
your big bird
in September.
Hugs & Pogo Sticks!
April

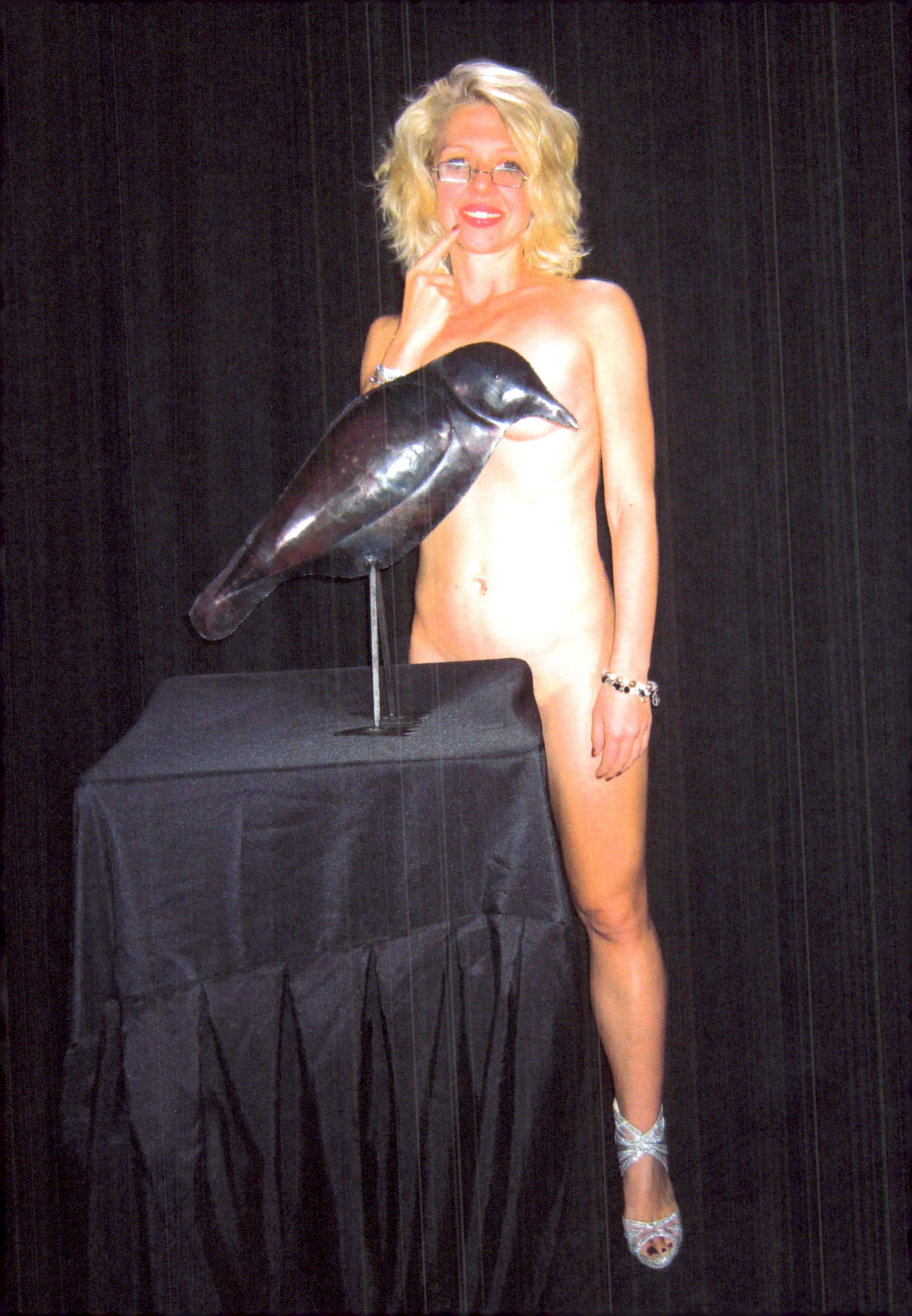

I dreamed
you were very bad
in October.
Hasta La Vista!
April

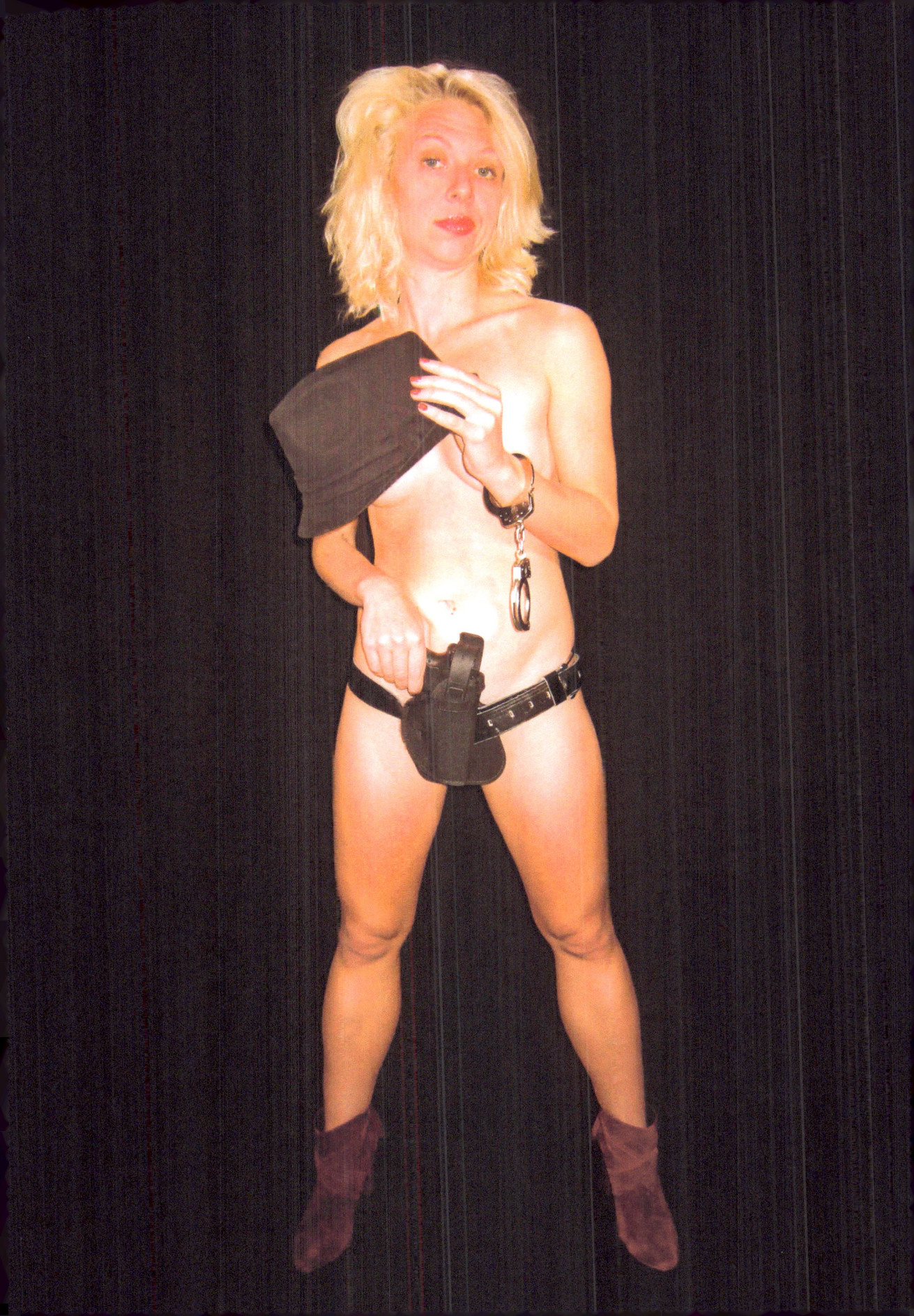

I dreamed
you watched
my show in
November.
Stay Tuned!
April

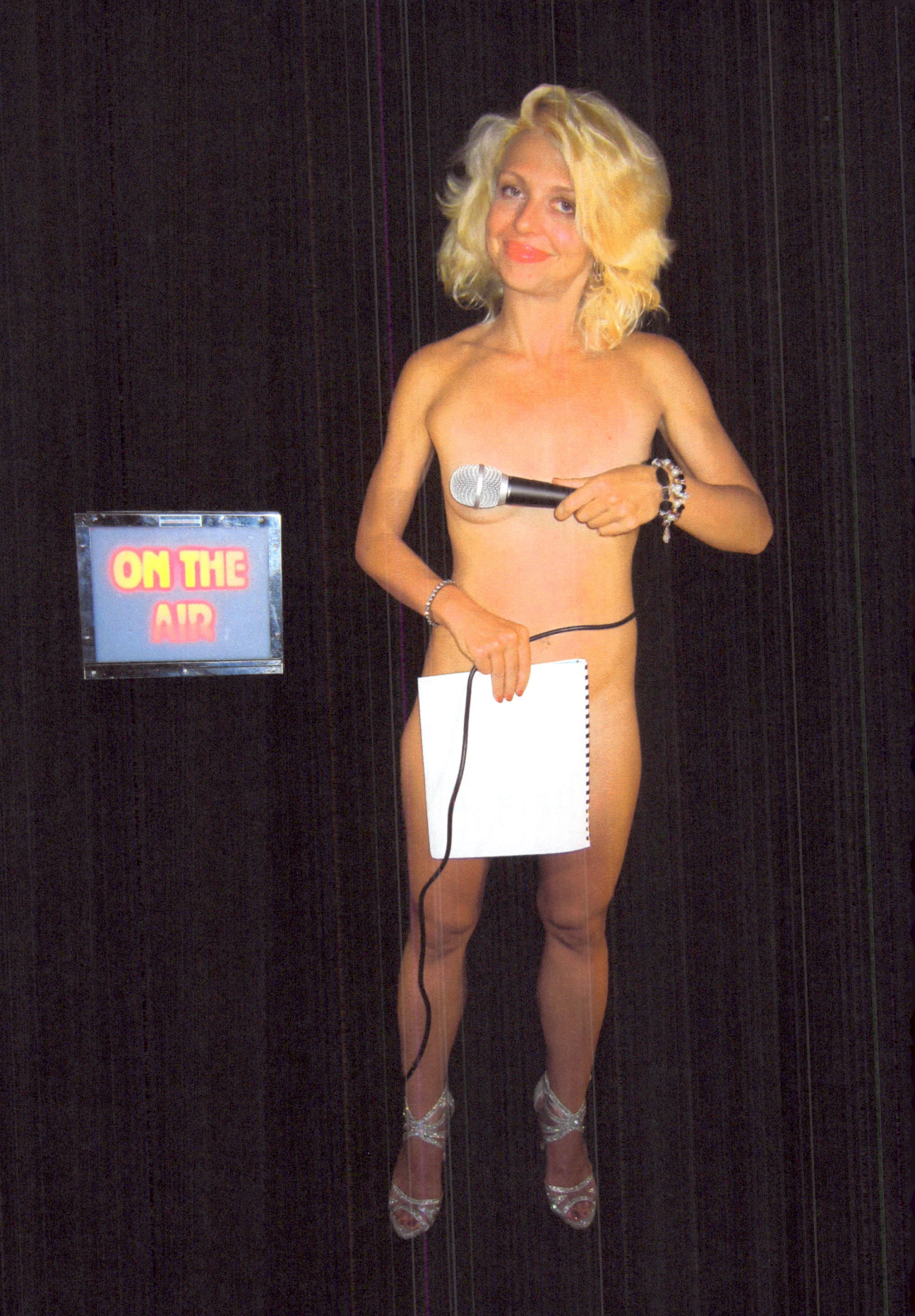

I dreamed you jingled my bells in December. Ho Ho Ho! April

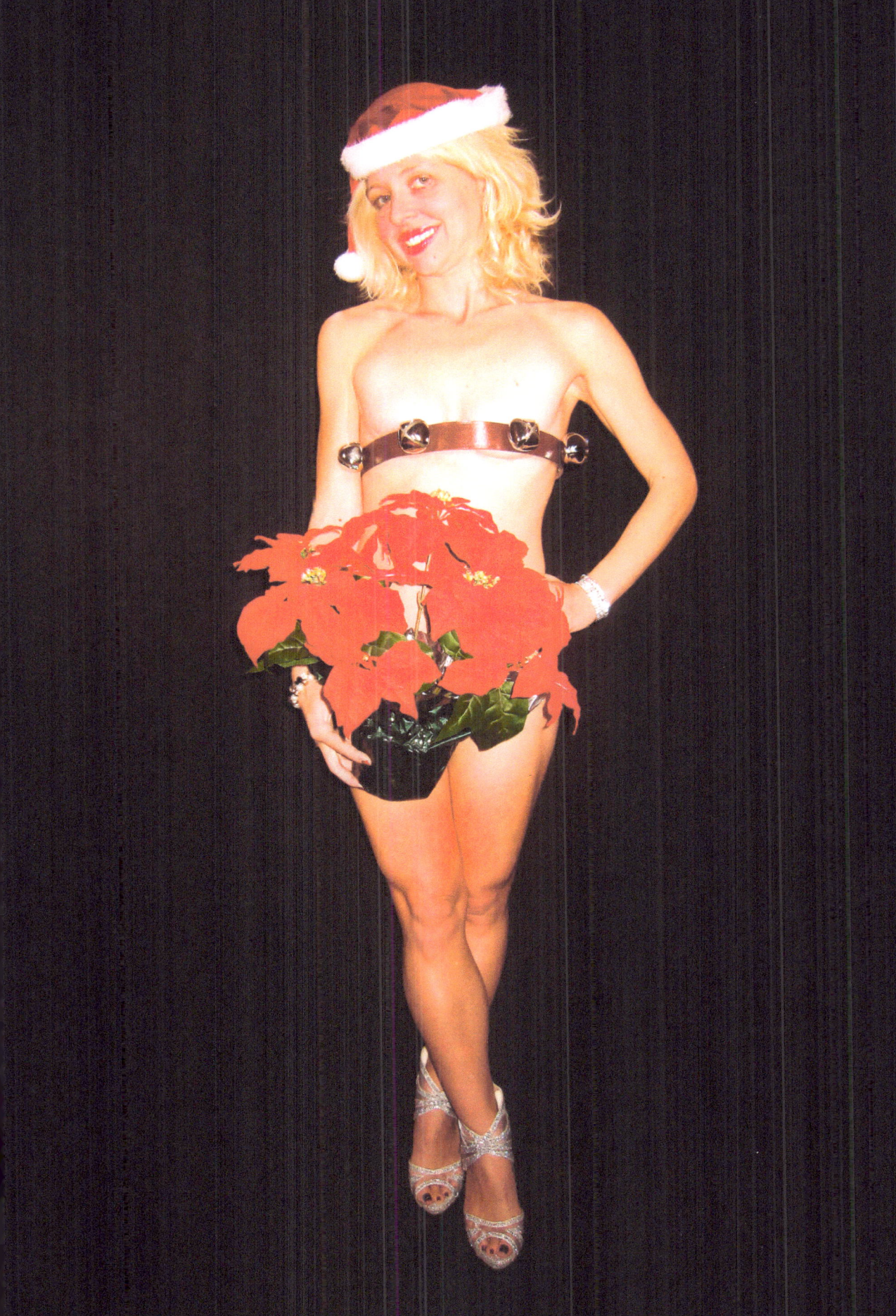

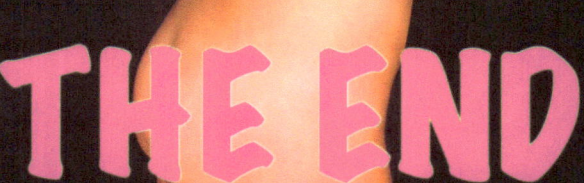

www.ingramcontent.com/pod-product-compliance
Lightning Source LLC
Chambersburg PA
CBHW050424180526
45159CB00005B/2402